AMY-

MW00987477

SIGNS *and* WONDERS

A BEGINNER'S GUIDE *to the* MIRACLES OF JESUS

Leader Guide
by Mike Poteet

Abingdon Press | Nashville

Signs and Wonders
A Beginner's Guide to the Miracles of Jesus
Leader Guide

Copyright © 2022 Amy-Jill Levine
All rights reserved.

978-1-7910-0770-6

MANUFACTURED IN THE UNITED STATES OF AMERICA

Contents

INTRODUCTION

In *Signs and Wonders*, Dr. Amy-Jill Levine (she prefers to be called AJ) invites readers to consider, wrestle with, and find new meaning in six Gospel stories about the miracles of Jesus.

This Leader Guide is designed to help small groups engage these stories, using AJ's insights into the texts' historical and cultural background, as well as her incisive and provocative questions about them, as springboards for their own discussions of what these texts meant and continue to mean, for them as individuals and for their communities of faith.

Rather than focusing on the texts' historicity—in other words, whether or not these miracles "really happened"—AJ approaches them as stories rich in detail, in resonance with Israel's Scriptures (the Christian Old Testament), and in emotional and spiritual truth.

This guide's six sessions correspond to the six chapters of *Signs and Wonders*:

- Session 1–"Take up your pallet and walk" (Mark 2:1-12)
- Session 2–Stilling the Storm (Mark 4:35-41)
- Session 3–The Feeding the Five Thousand (or More) (Luke 9:10-17)
- Session 4–A Bleeding Woman and a Dead Girl (Matthew 9:18-26)
- Session 5–A Two-Stage Miracle (Mark 8:22-26)
- Session 6 –The Raising of Lazarus (11:1-44)

Each session contains the following elements to draw from as you plan six in-person, virtual, or hybrid sessions (see "Leading Virtual Small-Group Sessions," pages 9–14):

- **Session Objectives**
- **Biblical Foundation(s)**—Scripture texts for the session, in the New Revised Standard Version.
- **Before Your Session**—Tips to help you prepare for a productive session.
- **Starting Your Session**—A suggested activity or guided discussion to introduce participants to the session's topic and to "warm them up" for conversation. Always be prepared to answer any questions you pose first, to set an example and to spark discussion. This section always includes the option of an opening prayer.
- **Discussion Questions**—These questions can guide you and your group through the Biblical Foundations. Most incorporate text from *Signs and Wonders*, so that even participants who have not read the book will be able fully to participate. You will likely not use all the suggested questions—you may not have enough time, you may judge some questions irrelevant to or inappropriate for your group, or your group may prefer a more freewheeling format. Select the questions you think will help your group the most.
- **Closing Your Session**—Suggestions for a focused discussion or brief activity to help participants move from reading and reflection to action after the session. This section also always includes the option of a closing prayer.
- **Optional Extensions**—One or more ways to continue discussion on the session's topics.

May this study spur your participants and you personally not only to a greater appreciation of the Gospel miracle stories, but also to a heightened sensitivity to God's miraculous ways in the world and in your community of faith. Thank you for your leadership!

Leading Virtual Small-Group Sessions

Meeting online is a great option for a number of situations. During a public-health hazard, such as the COVID-19 pandemic, online meetings are a welcome opportunity for people to converse while seeing each other's faces. Online meetings can also expand the "neighborhood" of group members, because people can log in from just about anywhere in the world. Online gatherings also give those who do not have access to transportation or who prefer not to travel at certain times of day the chance to participate.

The guidelines below will help you lead an effective and enriching group study using an online video conferencing platform.

Basic Features for Virtual Meetings

There are many choices for videoconferencing platforms. You may have personal experience and comfort using a particular service, or your church may have a subscription that will influence your choice. Whichever option you choose, it is recommended that you use a platform that supports the following features:

- **Synchronous video and audio:** Participants can see and speak to each other in real time. Participants have the ability to turn their video off and on, and to mute and unmute their audio.
- **Chat:** Participants can send messages to the whole group or to individuals within the virtual meeting. Participants can put active hyperlinks (for example, "clickable" internet addresses) into the chat for other participants' convenience.
- **Screen Sharing:** Participants can share the contents of their screen with other participants (the meeting host's permission may be required).
- **Video Sharing:** Participants (or the host) can share videos and computer audio via screen share, so that all participants can view the each week's videos.

- **Breakout Rooms:** Meeting hosts can automatically or manually send participants into virtual smaller groups, and they can determine whether or not participants will return to the main group automatically after a set period of time. Hosts can communicate with all breakout rooms. This feature is useful if your group is large or if you wish to break into teams of two or three for certain activities.

Check with your church administration to see if there is a preferred platform or an account that you might use. In most instances, only the host will need to be signed in to the account; others can participate without being registered.

Zoom, Webex, Google Meet, and Microsoft Teams all offer free versions of their platform, which you can use if your church doesn't have an account. However, there may be restrictions (for instance, Zoom's free version limits meetings to forty-five minutes). Check each platform's website to be sure you are aware of any such restrictions before you sign up.

Once you have selected a platform, familiarize yourself with all of its features and controls so that you can facilitate virtual meetings comfortably. The platform's website will have lists of features and helpful tutorials, and often third-party sites will have useful information or instructions as well.

In addition to videoconferencing software, it is also advisable to have access to slide-creation software such as Microsoft PowerPoint or Google Slides. These can be used to prepare slides for screen-sharing to display discussion questions, quotes from the study book, or Scripture passages. You can also create a document to share—just make sure the print size is easy to read.

Video Sharing

For a video-based study, it's important to be able to screen-share your videos so that all participants can view them in your study session. The good news is, whether you have the videos on DVD or streaming files, it is possible to play them in your session.

All of the videoconferencing platforms mentioned above support screen-sharing videos. Some have requirements for assuring that sound will play clearly in addition to the videos. Follow your videoconferencing platform instructions carefully and test the video sharing in advance to be sure it works.

If you wish to screen-share a DVD video, you may need to use a different media player. Some media players will not allow you to share your screen when you play copyright-protected DVDs. VLC is a free media player that is safe and easy to use. To try this software, download at videolan.org/VLC.

What about copyright? DVDs like those you use for group study are meant to be used in a group setting "real time." That is, whether you meet in person, online, or in a hybrid setting, Abingdon Press encourages use of your DVD or streaming video.

What is allowed: Streaming an Abingdon DVD over Zoom, Teams, or similar platform during a small group session.

What is not allowed: Posting video of a published DVD study to social media or YouTube for later viewing.

If you have any questions about permissions and copyright, email permissions@abingdonpress.com.

Amplify Media. The streaming subscription platform Amplify Media makes it easy to share streaming videos for groups. When your church has an Amplify subscription, your group members can sign on and have access to the video sessions. With access, they can watch the video on their own ahead of your group meeting, watch the video during your group meeting, or view the video again after the meeting. Thousands of videos are on AmplifyMedia.com; they are easy to watch anytime, anywhere, and on any device from phones and tablets to Smart TVs and desktops.

Visit AmplifyMedia.com to learn more or call 1-800-672-1789, option 4, to hear about the current offers.

Communicating with Your Group

Clear communication with your small group before and throughout your study is crucial no matter how you meet, and it is doubly important if you are gathering virtually.

Advertising the Study. Be sure to advertise your virtual study on your church's website and/or in its newsletter, as well as any social media that your church uses. Request pastors or other worship leaders announce it in worship services.

Registration. Encourage people to register for the online study so that you can know all participants and have a way to contact them. Ideally, you will collect email addresses for each participant so that you can send communications and links to your virtual meeting sessions. An event planning tool such as SignUpGenius makes this easy, and it gives you a database of participants and their email addresses.

Welcome Email. Before your first session, several days in advance, send an email to everyone registered for the study, welcoming them to the group, reminding them of the date and time of your first meeting, and including a link to join the virtual meeting. It's also a good idea to include one or two discussion questions to "prime the pump" for reflection and conversation when you gather.

If you have members without internet service, or if they are uncomfortable using a computer and videoconferencing software, let them know they may telephone into the meeting. Provide them the number and let them know that there is usually a unique phone number for each meeting.

Weekly Emails. Send a new email two or three days before each week's session, again including the link to your virtual meeting and one or two discussion questions to set the stage for discussion. Feel free to use any of the questions in the Leader Guide for this purpose. If you find a quote from the book that is especially meaningful, include this as well.

Facebook. Consider creating a private Facebook group for your small group. Here you can both have discussion and invite reflection between your weekly meetings. Each week, post one or two quotes from the study book along with a short question for reflection, and invite people to respond. These questions can come straight from the Leader Guide, and you can revisit the Facebook conversation during your virtual meeting.

You might also consider posting these quotes and questions on your church's Facebook page, inviting people in your congregation beyond your small group to join the conversation. This is a great way to let people know about your study and to invite them to join your next virtual meeting.

During Your Virtual Sessions

During your virtual sessions, follow these tips to be sure you are prepared and that everything runs as smoothly as possible.

- Familiarize yourself with the controls and features of your videoconferencing platform, using instructions or tutorials available via the platform's website or third-party sites.
- Be sure you are leading the session from a well-lit place in front of a background free from excessive distractions.
- As leader, log into the virtual meeting early. You want to be a good host who welcomes participants by name as they arrive. Logging in early also gives you time to check how you appear on camera, so that you can make last-minute adjustments to your lighting and background if needed.
- During each session, pay attention to who is speaking and who is not. Because of video and audio lags as well as internet connections of varying quality, some participants may inadvertently speak over each other without realizing they are doing so. As needed, directly prompt specific people to speak if they wish (for example, "Alan, it looked like you were about to say something when Sarah was speaking").

- If your group is large, you may want to agree with members on a procedure for being recognized to speak (for example, participants might "raise hands" digitally or type "call on me" in the chat feature).
- Instruct participants to keep their microphones muted during the meeting to avoid extraneous noise that can interrupt discussion. This includes chewing or yawning sounds, which can be embarrassing! When it is time for discussion, participants can unmute themselves.
- Remember that some participants may wish simply to observe and listen—do not pressure anyone to speak.
- Always get your group's permission before recording your online sessions. While those who are unable to attend the meeting may appreciate the chance to view it later, respect the privacy of your participants.

In challenging times, modern technology has powerful potential to bring God's people together in new and nourishing ways. May such be your experience during this virtual study.

SESSION 1

"Take up your pallet and walk"
On the Role of Caregivers
(Mark 2:1-12)

Session Objectives

Through this session's readings and discussion, participants will:

- articulate their understandings of "miracle" and identify their attitudes toward biblical stories about miracles, especially Jesus's miracles;
- name caregivers who have served them, as well as ways in which they have served as caregivers;
- study what Mark 2:1-12 has to say about physical caregiving, spiritual caregiving, and connections between the two; and
- identify present and future ways their community of faith is or could become a "Capernaum"—a place of caregiving and healing.

Biblical Foundation

When [Jesus] returned to Capernaum after some days, it was reported that he was at home. So many gathered around that there was no longer room for them, not even in front of the door; and he was speaking the word to them. Then some people came, bringing to him a paralyzed man, carried by four of them. And when they could not bring him to Jesus because of the crowd, they removed the roof above him; and after having dug through it, they let down the mat on which the paralytic lay. When Jesus saw their faith, he said to the paralytic, "Son, your sins are forgiven." Now some of the scribes were sitting there, questioning in their hearts, "Why does this fellow speak in this way? It is blasphemy! Who can forgive sins but God alone?" At once Jesus perceived in his spirit that they were discussing these questions among themselves; and he said to them, "Why do you raise such questions in your hearts? Which is easier, to say to the paralytic, 'Your sins are forgiven,' or to say, 'Stand up and take your mat and walk'? But so that you may know that the Son of Man has authority on earth to forgive sins"—he said to the paralytic—"I say to you, stand up, take your mat and go to your home." And he stood up, and immediately took the mat and went out before all of them; so that they were all amazed and glorified God, saying, "We have never seen anything like this!"

Mark 2:1-12

Before Your Session

- Carefully read the introduction and chapter 1 of *Signs and Wonders*, noting topics about which you have questions or want to do further research.
- Read this session's Biblical Foundation several times, as well as background information about it from a trusted study Bible or commentary.
- You will need: Bibles for participants and/or on-screen slides, prepared with Scripture texts, to share; newsprint or a markerboard and markers if you are meeting in person.

Starting Your Session

Welcome participants and tell them why you are excited about studying *Signs and Wonders* with them. Invite participants to talk briefly about why they are interested in this study and what they would like to gain from it. Ask:

- What's the most amazing thing you've ever seen or experienced?
- How do you define "miracle"?
- How do you find the word "miracle" used in everyday conversation?
- What, if anything, have you seen or experienced yourself that you would call a miracle? Why?
- Do you know people who have or say they have experienced a miracle? What happened?
- In general, how do you react to stories about miracles in the Bible, and why?
- In *Signs and Wonders*, AJ states, "Either we believe in miracles of the sort the Gospels describe, or we don't. But—and here's the good news—for the stories to have value for us, the question of historicity [in other words, whether the miracles actually happened] is not of ultimate import." Do you agree? Why or why not?

Brainstorm with participants a list of Jesus's miracles as described in the Gospels. Write their responses on newsprint or markerboard, and/or your video conferencing platform's "whiteboard" feature. Invite participants to talk about how they have seen and heard these miracles depicted outside Scripture—in hymns and other music, artwork, films, and so on.

Read aloud from *Signs and Wonders*:

> Pretty much everyone [in the ancient world] agreed that miracles occurred; the question was what they signified.... If our major sense of Jesus is "great miracle worker," we've missed the point of the New Testament.

- Ask: "What are some things you think Jesus's miracles signify?" Write participants' responses. Refer back to and add to this list as your group's study continues.

Read aloud from *Signs and Wonders*:

> [T]he stories [about Jesus's miracles] still have power. They project us into a world where amazement is possible. Like parables, they help us see the world otherwise.

Encourage participants to notice, throughout your study, what new thoughts and feelings these stories prompt for them about the world, about Jesus and God, and about the nature and mission of God's people.

Lead this prayer aloud, or use one of your own:

Mighty God, whenever we turn to the Scriptures, we ask a miracle: that we hear these ancient words as fresh, powerful teachings from You. As we study these stories of Jesus, amaze us with his compassion, his commitment to Your will, and his continuing call for us to live as Your children. May his wonderful works make us bold to do the works to which You call us, and for which You have claimed us in him. Amen.

Discussion Questions

Meeting Caregivers in Capernaum

Discuss:

- When you think about caregivers, what images or people come to mind?
- How is caregiving both, in AJ's words, "an emotional investment" and "an ethical imperative"?
- What is the relationship between caring for others and caring for oneself?

"Take up your pallet and walk"

Recruit one or more volunteers to read aloud Mark 2:1-12, while other participants follow along silently in their Bibles. Discuss:

- Why is the crowd in Capernaum gathering around Jesus (verses 1-2)?
- Mark's early focus, writes AJ, "is not on the man" who is paralyzed but "on the health care workers" who get him in front of Jesus (verses 3-4). What questions do you have about "these bed-bearers"?
- Mark doesn't give us more information about them—what else about them would you like to know?
- AJ asks, "Who carried us when we could not carry ourselves?" Who in your life has carried you, literally or figuratively? Whom have you carried? What advantages and limitations, if any, does "carrying" offer as an image of caregiving?
- "On the ethical level," AJ writes, "the story tells us that, to find a healing, one does what one can, even if it means tearing down whatever barrier is keeping us from obtaining the healing." What barriers have stood or still stand between you or those you know, and healing? What barriers does society put up between healing and those who most need it? What responsibility does the community of faith bear for "digging through" those barriers?
- Jesus sees the "faith" of those who got the man into the house (verse 5). AJ asks, "Faith in what?" How do you answer? Why?
- Citing James 2:26, AJ states "faith is something less that you 'believe' and more something that you 'do.'" Do you agree? Why or why not?
- "I want the efforts of the caregivers to be acknowledged," writes AJ. "So often, even today, they are not." Which caregivers, within or beyond its own membership, does your congregation acknowledge, and how? When has

caregiving you've provided gone unacknowledged, and how did you react?

- Does your church have a caregiving team or other group of people who with the clergy attend to people in need of care? Do you know what they do? Do you know who they are?

- Noting that Mark doesn't tell the name of the man who is paralyzed, AJ writes, "In Gospel healing narratives, we do not get the names of those to whom Jesus bestows health care; instead, we have people-as-symptoms." When, if ever, have you been identified as your "symptoms"? Who, if anyone, do you tend to identify as their "symptoms"? How do we avoid reducing anyone to what we may perceive as their "weakness" or "handicap"?

- Jesus's first word to the man can be translated "son" or (as AJ argues, more accurately) "child" (verse 5). What does this address to the man imply about how Jesus views their relationship? How easily do you think of yourself as a "son," "daughter," or "child" of Jesus? How readily do you think of others—especially those society identifies by their "symptoms"—in that way? How might Genesis 1:27; Mark 3:35; John 20:16-17; or Hebrews 2:11-15 add to this discussion?

- "I suspect," writes AJ, "that at some point we all yearn to be children again.... We speak of being 'babied,' but that's not necessarily a bad thing (as long as we don't make a habit of it)." Do you agree? Why or why not? How can a yearning to be a child who is cared for shape the ways we give care to others? Are there ways in which it should not?

- AJ speculates on how the man who was paralyzed lived his life after Jesus healed him. How have your experiences of being cared for changed you? How have they influenced your readiness to care for other people?

Forgiving Sins as Spiritual Caregiving

Read aloud from *Signs and Wonders*:

> Mark is such a remarkable storyteller: our focus is now on
> the question of forgiveness of sin.... [S]uddenly the health
> care is interrupted with a theological debate.

Discuss:

- AJ points out "the dominant first-century Jewish view"
  was *not* that "disability is the result of sin." Neither the
  man who is paralyzed nor those who bring him before
  Jesus ask for forgiveness of sins. Why, then, do you think
  that Jesus pronounces the man's sins forgiven? (See also
  Mark 1:14-15.)
- Mark doesn't tell us what sins the man has committed, or
  whether the man repented of his sins once Jesus declared
  them forgiven. What do you make of this silence? Does it
  matter whether the man has repented?
- When, in your own or others' experience, have you seen
  "a positive response" to "[f]orgiveness, given graciously,
  with no strings attached"? What are the risks, if any, of
  extending such forgiveness? What are the risks, if any, in
  not extending it?
- Why does Jesus use the passive rather than the active
  voice in pronouncing the man's sins forgiven ("Your sins
  are forgiven," not "I forgive your sins")? How do his words
  undercut the charge of "blasphemy" some scribes level
  against Jesus in their hearts (verses 6-7)?
- AJ thinks one reason the scribes' reaction upsets Jesus is
  that "they do not say what they are thinking," which "can
  be a type of hypocrisy." How, if at all, do you imagine
  this encounter might have unfolded differently had the
  scribes spoken directly to Jesus? How do we discern when
  speaking up about what angers us is the caring thing to

do, and when it isn't? Can you give an example of when you saw something you thought was wrong but did not speak up?

- AJ writes: "It is one thing to proclaim 'you are forgiven'; it is something else to feel it." When have you felt truly forgiven? When do you feel you have truly forgiven someone else? Does pronouncing or hearing forgiveness when we may not feel it deeply, or at all, have value? Why or why not?

- "The greater miracle in terms of spectacle," AJ writes, is the man who was paralyzed standing up and walking, but "for those who feel the burden of sin...the greater miracle is forgiveness." When have you witnessed the miracle of forgiveness, in your own or another's life?

- AJ states "to forgive is *not* to forget." What does she mean? Do you agree? Why or why not?

Closing Your Session: Acting as a "Capernaum" Community of Care

Recruit a volunteer to read aloud Mark 1:21-28—the first time Jesus is in Capernaum in Mark's Gospel—while other participants read along silently.

Discuss:

- How might Jesus's earlier visit to Capernaum help us find even more meaning in his second, which we've studied today? Refer to AJ's discussion of Mark 1:21-28 in chapter 1 as needed.

Tell participants that in Mark's Gospel, according to AJ, Capernaum—while always an actual village in first-century Galilee—also "becomes primarily a place of healing." It is the place where a community hears Jesus proclaim God's Word and experiences, through his miracles, God's care for those who need healing from whatever keeps them "from fully participating in the community." It is a place where, in AJ's words, "Any house can be a synagogue, and any house, or synagogue, can be a hospital."

Discuss:

- Where are or where have been the "Capernaums," the places of healing, in your life?
- Would you identify your congregation as a place of healing? Would other people? Why or why not?
- In what practical and specific ways does your congregation seek to serve as a place of healing the whole person—physical, emotional, mental, and spiritual?
- What more might your congregation do to become a "Capernaum" for those who need healing the most?

Close by leading this prayer aloud, or one of your own:

Heal us, O God, of all that would keep us from living as Your children. Heal us of all that keeps us from caring for our neighbors as You have commanded and from caring for ourselves as we must. Heal us of guilt and regret, resentment and hate, and all that keeps us from moving forward in faith and hope. And heal us from all that stops us from asking, in Your name and to Your glory, "What can we do to help?" Amen.

Optional Extensions

- Compare and contrast Mark 2:1-12 with John 5:1-17, as AJ does. How does each story help us understand the other better?
- Find paintings or statues that depict this scene—does the artist's vision match the pictures it evokes in your mind?
- Invite an essential health care worker (if your group does not already include one or more) to participate in your discussion of caregiving.

SESSION 2

Stilling the Storm
Attending to Nature
(Mark 4:35-41)

Session Objectives

Through this session's readings and discussion, participants will:

- reflect on how the biblical tradition shapes our attitudes toward the natural world;
- listen to and closely read the story of Jesus stilling a storm in Mark 4, asking it questions about Jesus's identity, the responsibilities of disciples, and the nature of trust; and
- explore how biblical lamentation offers a way of responding to the mystery of why God does not still all storms, literal and otherwise, in this world.

Biblical Foundations

By awesome deeds you answer us with deliverance,
*   O God of our salvation;*
you are the hope of all the ends of the earth
*   and of the farthest seas.*
By your strength you established the mountains;
*   you are girded with might.*

Stilling the Storm

You silence the roaring of the seas,
the roaring of their waves,
the tumult of the peoples.
Those who live at earth's farthest bounds are awed by your
signs;
you make the gateways of the morning and the evening
shout for joy.

Psalm 65:5-8

But as for me, my prayer is to you, O LORD.
At an acceptable time, O God,
in the abundance of your steadfast love, answer me.
With your faithful help rescue me
from sinking in the mire;
let me be delivered from my enemies
and from the deep waters.
Do not let the flood sweep over me,
or the deep swallow me up,
or the Pit close its mouth over me.
Answer me, O LORD, for your steadfast love is good;
according to your abundant mercy, turn to me.

Psalm 69:13-16

On that day, when evening had come, [Jesus] said to [his disciples], "Let us go across to the other side." And leaving the crowd behind, they took him with them in the boat, just as he was. Other boats were with him. A great windstorm arose, and the waves beat into the boat, so that the boat was already being swamped. But he was in the stern, asleep on the cushion; and they woke him up and said to him, "Teacher, do you not care that we are perishing?" He woke up and rebuked the wind, and said to the sea, "Peace! Be still!" Then the wind ceased, and there was a dead calm. He said to them, "Why are you afraid? Have you still no faith?" And they were filled with great awe and said to one another, "Who then is this, that even the wind and the sea obey him?"

Mark 4:35-41

Before Your Session

- Carefully read chapter 2 of *Signs and Wonders*, noting topics about which you have questions or want to do further research.
- Read this session's Biblical Foundations several times, as well as background information about them from a trusted study Bible or commentary.
- You will need: Bibles for participants and/or on-screen slides, prepared with Scripture texts, to share; on-site gatherings will need newsprint or a markerboard and markers.
- *Optional*: Ask participants to find an impressive image of the natural world to share (be sure to find one yourself too).
- *Optional*: Recruit someone to prepare to read Mark 4:35-41, with attention to meaning and emotion.

Starting Your Session

Welcome participants.

Invite volunteers to talk briefly about a time they have been impressed by the natural world—its beauty and variety, its scale and power. *Optional*: Invite participants to find and share images of nature (starting with those you asked to be ready to share). (If using a video conference platform, be sure to enable participants' ability to share their screens.)

Discuss:

- At the start of chapter 2 of *Signs and Wonders*, AJ discusses how arguments that the Bible and Judaism denigrate nature by subordinating it to God rang false for her. Do you think the Bible encourages people to respect or to disrespect nature? Why? In your experience, how much does Christian faith and practice encourage care for the natural world?

- Scriptures like Genesis 1:26-30, Psalm 8, and Wisdom of Solomon 9:1-3 (Deuterocanonical/Apocryphal) claim God has given human beings "dominion" over the world God created. AJ asserts this "dominion" means "our job is to protect nature and to celebrate the gifts it provides, not to destroy it." How do we tell the difference between "dominion over" and "domination of" nature? How are you and your congregation practicing dominion instead of domination?
- AJ notes the Jewish festivals Passover, Shavuot (Festival of Weeks), and Sukkot (Festival of Booths) all began as agricultural celebrations, and points to the Jewish holiday Tu b'Shevat "as a type of Arbor Day or Earth Day." What holidays and celebrations, if any, help you remember our connections to nature? How does or how could the church "recover attention to the world of nature" in its festivals?
- AJ says biblical tradition helps us see that nature testifies to the divine "while it is not itself divine." How important a distinction is this one to draw? Why?

Tell participants that the miracle story in this session encourages us to attend both to nature and to God.

Lead this prayer aloud, or offer one of your own:

Creator God, how countless are Your works! In wisdom You made them all. You filled the earth with Your creatures and entrusted us, Your human creatures, with responsibility for them; yet You alone rule us all. As we read and study another story of Jesus's miracles today, fill us with wise regard for the forces of nature and deeper reverence for You, whom even the wind and the sea obey. Amen.

Discussion Questions

Studying Jesus's Stilling of a Storm

Ask participants to keep their Bibles closed for the moment. You, or someone you have recruited beforehand, should read aloud

Mark 4:35-41, attending to the meaning and emotions of the text. After this presentation, and before they open their Bibles (or look at the text on a prepared slide), ask participants what words, images, or other details most caught their attention. Always assure participants you aren't looking for "right answers" but are trying to help them approach what will be, for many, a familiar text in a new way.

Now have participants turn to the story in their Bibles. Discuss:

- AJ notes the story begins after "that day" (verse 35) of Jesus teaching the crowds in parables and wonders whether the stilling of the storm is itself "a type of parable" that, like all parables, "helps us to see the world and ourselves in a different light." What do you think, and why?
- On "the other side" of the lake is the Decapolis, "a series of ten Greek states with a broadly Gentile population." What significance do you find in Jesus suggesting this destination to his disciples? Consider AJ's statements that "Jews did not despise Gentiles" and that "Jesus did not invent universalism" when pondering reasons for Jesus's travel plan.
- AJ notes that Jesus "is actually commanding, but in a way that also suggests that the disciples have a choice." Why do you think his disciples agree with his suggestion? What happened when you went somewhere because someone else suggested the trip? When, if ever, have you gone somewhere you wouldn't necessarily have gone because you sensed God suggesting you go? What happened? Would you go back? Why or why not?
- Commenting on the disciples taking Jesus "just as he was" (verse 36), AJ suggests it means "they acted for him, because he was too tired to do much more on his own." How do you understand Mark's comment? Does this understanding of Jesus as fully human, and so fully tired, disturb you or comfort you? How does or how could your

congregation regularly care for people within and outside of your membership who are exhausted and "wiped"?

- What do you make of Jesus sleeping through the storm (verses 37-38)? AJ suggests Jesus's sleep exemplifies trust in other people and in God. How so? Whom, if anyone, do you so trust that you feel you could have slept free from fear in their presence?

- "The storm, the sleeping hero, the desperate sailors, even a voyage away from Jewish to Gentile territory, all connect the stories of Jonah and Jesus." Read Jonah 1. How do each of these two stories help you make sense of the other? How and why do Matthew and Luke connect Jesus with Jonah (Matthew 12:38-41; Luke 11:29-32)?

- Verse 38 is the first time anyone in Mark's Gospel calls Jesus "teacher"—unexpectedly and ironically, says AJ, because Jesus isn't actively teaching but sleeping at that moment! What important things does the title "teacher" say about Jesus? What important things about him does it left unsaid? How important to you personally is "teacher" as a name or title for Jesus? Why?

- "Out on the ocean," writes AJ, "in the dark, in the storm, and worse is the sense that God is not only asleep but also doesn't care." When have you or when has someone you know asked God the disciples' question, "Do you not care?" What answer came, if any? What would you tell— or what have you told—someone who confides in you, "I worry God doesn't care"?

- Since, as AJ notes, at least four of Jesus's dozen closest disciples were fishermen, she sees the disciples as failing to "take the lead" and "abdicat[ing] their responsibility" in the storm. Do you agree? Why or why not? When, if ever, have you failed to "take the lead" in a situation where your gifts and talents might have made a difference? When, if ever, have you discovered previously unknown gifts and talents by unexpectedly "taking the lead"? In your experience, how quick are believers to assume they can do nothing in a situation *but* call on God? Why?

- AJ points out the Greek verb describing Jesus's waking in verse 39 is a form of the same verb with which Mark describes Jesus's resurrection (16:6). What significance, if any, do you find in this detail? How does it affect your reading of this story?

- AJ states Jesus's words to the storm are best translated, "Silence, shut up!" How does the "crudeness" of this translation (as opposed to the more polite, "Peace! Be still!") shape your view of Jesus? What can Jesus's followers learn from the blunt way he speaks to the storm?

- Mark says Jesus "rebuked" the storm. Compare Mark's use of the same verb in 1:25, 8:31-32, and 9:25. What might Jesus's "rebuke" of this storm suggest about its origin and purpose?

- Read Psalm 65:5-8. AJ cites other Scriptures emphasizing God's control over wind and waves (Psalms 89:9-10, 107:23-30; Isaiah 51:9-11). What does Mark's echoing of these Scriptures suggest he believes is the answer to the disciples' question in verse 41?

- AJ translates Jesus's question to the disciples (verse 40) as, "Do you not yet have trust?" How do you understand the relationship between faith and trust? How could the disciples have demonstrated trust in Jesus during this storm? How do you, or how would you like to, demonstrate such trust during the storms that arise in your and your congregation's life?

Closing Your Session: Lamenting the Other Boats

AJ highlights an intriguing detail in Mark's narrative: "other boats were with" Jesus (verse 36). We never learn what stories people in those other boats had to tell after the storm. Remembering her grandfather who died at sea, AJ writes, "Not everyone has Jesus asleep in the boat; not every wind is stilled."

Biblical lamentation, several examples of which AJ cites in chapter 2, may help us respond to the mystery of why some storms are rebuked while others aren't, why some boats reach safe harbor while others don't.

Recruit volunteers to read aloud Psalm 69 (or at least verses 13-16), while others follow along silently. Discuss:

- How would you describe the psalmist's tone? How does it change over the course of the psalm?
- How was the disciples' cry to Jesus like and unlike a lamentation?
- What storms in your life, in your congregation's life, or in the world make you want to lament to God? Have you? Why or why not?
- How might lamenting the danger these storms pose be an important ministry for communities of faith?
- AJ says that the disciples "abdicate their responsibility...they rely on Jesus rather than on themselves." What active, embodied forms can lamentation take to keep us from abdicating our responsibility?

Close by leading this prayer aloud, or one of your own:

Awake, holy God, and save those who are in danger. Guide those who are lost in any kind of storm, over whom any flood threatens to sweep. With boldness as Your children, we plea for Your attention and Your aid. With humility as your servants, we ask for strength to minister to those in need in Your name. With gratitude, we trust in Your love and Your grace. Amen.

Alternatively, lead your group in a unison or responsive reading of Psalm 65:5-8 as a closing prayer.

Optional Extensions

- Invite someone (if one isn't already present in your group) who makes or made their living on the sea, or who has personally experienced a storm at sea, to participate in your discussion.
- Encourage participants to research, using trustworthy sources, how modern Jewish observance of Passover, Shavuot, Sukkot (Festival of Booths), and Tu b'Shevat encourages faithful attention to God's creation. Invite a rabbi or Jewish religious educator to talk about these festivals with your group.

SESSION 3

The Feeding of the Five Thousand (or More)
The Centrality of Bread
(Luke 9:10-17)

Session Objectives

Through this session's readings and discussion, participants will:

- share memories of significant meals in their lives, identifying several dimensions of meals' importance;
- discuss Old Testament stories of miraculous feedings as important background to Gospel accounts of Jesus's food miracles;
- read and discuss Luke's account of how Jesus miraculously provided food for five thousand men; and
- identify steps their congregation does and can take to address local food insecurity.

Biblical Foundation

On their return the apostles told Jesus all they had done. He took them with him and withdrew privately to a city called

Bethsaida. When the crowds found out about it, they followed him; and he welcomed them, and spoke to them about the kingdom of God, and healed those who needed to be cured.

The day was drawing to a close, and the twelve came to him and said, "Send the crowd away, so that they may go into the surrounding villages and countryside, to lodge and get provisions; for we are here in a deserted place." But he said to them, "You give them something to eat." They said, "We have no more than five loaves and two fish—unless we are to go and buy food for all these people." For there were about five thousand men. And he said to his disciples, "Make them sit down in groups of about fifty each." They did so and made them all sit down. And taking the five loaves and the two fish, he looked up to heaven, and blessed and broke them, and gave them to the disciples to set before the crowd. And all ate and were filled. What was left over was gathered up, twelve baskets of broken pieces.

Luke 9:10-17

Before Your Session

- Carefully read chapter 3 of *Signs and Wonders*, noting topics about which you have questions or want to do further research.
- Read this session's Biblical Foundation, as well as the Scriptures assigned in "Remembering Old Testament Food Miracles" of this session's activities several times, as well as background information about them from a trusted study Bible or commentary.
- You will need: Bibles for participants and/or on-screen slides, prepared with Scripture texts, to share; on-site gatherings will need newsprint or a markerboard and markers.
- Locate accurate, reliable information about food insecurity in your community, and be ready to share it with your group.

- Remember to lead discussions of food and food insecurity with sensitivity to group members who may not have enough to eat, who may be dealing with eating disorders, or whose relationship to food is otherwise complicated (as all our relationships to food are, in one way or other). Should you become aware of urgent issues members are facing, be ready to offer helpful resources.

Starting Your Session

Welcome participants.

Invite them to remember a favorite meal—whether from the past year or in their whole lives—that they can recall in some detail. Ask volunteers to talk briefly about what makes the meal so memorable. After several people have talked about their meals, discuss:

- What are some things our stories of memorable meals have in common?
- How much of what makes a meal memorable can people who prepare and provide the meal control? How much can those who consume the meal control?
- How do memorable meals nourish not only our bodies but also our hearts, minds, and spirits?

Tell participants the miracle story in this session recounts a meal so memorable, some form of it appears in all four Gospels— the only miracle to do so. It also echoes memorable meals from Israel's past, and it looks forward not only to the Last Supper, but also to the heavenly banquet.

Lead this prayer aloud, or one of your own:

Generous God, from whose loving hand all our food ultimately comes, feed us now with Your Word, that as we study, discuss, and digest the Scripture today, Your Spirit may strengthen us to live as Your ever more faithful people, for the sake of Jesus, who taught us to trust You for our daily bread. Amen.

Discussion Questions

Recalling Old Testament Food Miracles

Remind participants that stories about Jesus's miraculous feedings of crowds aren't the Bible's first food miracle stories. Form three groups of participants. Assign each group Scriptures to read and discuss:

- Exodus 16:1-5, 13-21
- 1 Kings 17:8-16
- 2 Kings 4:42-44

Small groups can gather in different areas of your meeting space or, if your group is using a videoconferencing platform, in virtual breakout rooms. Depending on your group's size, you may want or need to form only two small groups, with one studying Exodus 16 and the other the stories from Kings. If time allows, feel free to expand the selection from Exodus 16.

Give small groups these questions to use in discussing their stories. You will want to write these questions on newsprint or markerboard so participants can refer back to them, or share them in your video conferencing platform's chat feature. Let the groups know that they need not address every question.

- Where is this story set?
- Why is food lacking? How is it provided?
- To what do characters in this story object, and why? How are these objections addressed?
- What, if anything, beyond physical sustenance does food represent in this story?
- What claim(s) do you hear in this story about God, humanity, and their relationship?

Allow seven to ten minutes for small groups to read and discuss their stories. Reconvene the whole group. Invite a volunteer from each group to report a few highlights from their discussion.

Option: Summarize all three stories for your group, or recruit volunteers beforehand to prepare summaries to present.

Exploring Luke's Story of a Food Miracle

Recruit volunteers to read aloud Luke 9:10-17, while others read along silently. Discuss:

- As the story begins, from where are the apostles returning (verse 10), and what have they been doing (see 9:1-6)? How might this context shed light on the miracle about to occur?

- This feeding takes place shortly after Herod beheads John the Baptizer (9:7-9). Luke doesn't give the specifics Mark (6:18-28) and Matthew (14:4-11) do: Herod had John beheaded at the request of his wife's daughter, who danced for him at a feast. "Meals can be places of hate as well as hospitality," notes AJ. When have you experienced hate (even if not at such murderous heights) at a meal? How did you handle the situation?

- This miracle occurs in or near Bethsaida. What will Jesus say about Bethsaida (and other cities around the Sea of Galilee) in Luke 10:13-15? AJ suggests Luke 9:10 and 10:13 together make us "realize how fragile good news can be.... Then and now, people ask, 'What you done for me lately?'" Have you been aware of this tendency in your own faith? How do you resist it and renew your attention to God's good news?

- Jesus welcomes, teaches, and heals the crowd following him (verse 11). AJ identifies welcoming, teaching, and healing as three related actions that make up the "sense of mutual hospitality" surrounding Jesus and his followers. How does your congregation welcome, teach, and heal people, especially those new to your community? How well does your congregation balance these actions? Have you experienced genuinely mutual hospitality in a community not your own? In that other setting, were you ever ignored, or made to feel unwelcome? What could your congregation do to cultivate such hospitality?

- AJ wonders if, in ordering welcome, teaching, and healing as he does, "Luke shows how worship is done." Does your congregation's form of worship attend to these three actions? Does the order matter, and if so, why?

- As AJ explains, the apostles tell Jesus, literally, to "release" the crowd in verse 12 ("Send the crowd away," NRSV). What motivates this request? Do you have positive, negative, or mixed reactions to it, and why?

- Jesus, his apostles, and the crowd are "in a desert place." How does this setting evoke Israel's past (Exodus 16)? What expectations might this setting raise for those who know Israel's history with God? (See also 1 Kings 19:4-8.)

- How does the desert setting evoke John the Baptizer's ministry (Luke 3:1-6), and what might those connections mean for Jesus and his followers?

- How does the desert setting evoke Jesus's own past (Luke 4:1-4)? Why does Jesus not miraculously produce food in Luke 4 as he does in Luke 9?

- "The disciples' invocation gives a sense of economic prosperity," notes AJ—a perhaps "too optimistic" assumption that those in the crowd could find food and lodging on their own. Have you heard similar assumptions? How do we check our tendency, in AJ's words, to "take for granted that the things we easily purchase are within reach of others"?

- AJ allows that the disciples may also have expected the crowds would encounter hospitality on the road as they themselves had on their mission (9:4). Do you find "the idea that people will provide hospitality to strangers" today "extraordinary," as AJ does? Why or why not? How easily do you extend hospitality to strangers? What considerations do you weigh?

- "Jesus's command, 'You give them something to eat,' is both direct and opaque." How so? With what tone of voice do you hear the apostles' responding—genuine willingness? Snarky push-back, as AJ suggests? Something else?

- AJ states the apostles "do not want, or do not think, they have the capacity to do anything for the crowds.... Had they realized the gifts they had already been given... they should not have been shocked." When faced with other people's needs, how do you and your congregation take stock of the gifts you have been given and that you can offer? How clearly do your congregational budget and your own checkbook reflect the extent of your capacity to aid other people in need?

- Luke's headcount of the crowd is five thousand men (verse 14; contrast Matthew 14:21). AJ finds this apparently "gender-segregated crowd" consistent with Luke's tendency "to relegate [women] to ancillary positions." What challenges can Luke's Gospel and our society offer each other regarding gender roles?

- AJ doesn't find attempts to ascribe symbolism to the number of loaves and fish convincing or helpful. Do you? Why or why not?

- Read Luke 22:19-20 and 24:28-31. How do Jesus's actions in feeding the five thousand anticipate his Last Supper and the supper at Emmaus? Do you find these similarities significant? If so, how so?

- Jesus gives food to his disciples to distribute (verse 16; compare Mark 6:41 and Matthew 14:19; contrast John 6:11). Why do you think Jesus involves his followers in getting the food to the people?
- Contrary to often heard "explanations" of this miracle, AJ states, "This is no 'shared meal.'" How and why does Luke make the miraculous nature of this meal clear?

Closing Your Session: Attention to Food Insecurity

Read aloud from *Signs and Wonders*:

> Rather than hear the crowd's reaction [to Jesus's miracle], we feel what they feel: they were "filled." For people with food insecurity, that would be a great miracle. For people who have more than enough, the story reminds us that not everyone does.

Briefly present the information you gathered before your session about food insecurity in your community. Discuss ways in which your congregation does and could do more to help people who need food. Identify at least one practical next step your group will take to address local food insecurity.

Close by leading this prayer aloud, or one of your own:

Lord Jesus, Bread of Life, You tell us, who would follow You, "Give them something to eat." May we obey Your command with eagerness and joy, trusting You to fill empty stomachs through our faithful responses. May every meal we provide for others and every meal we eat not only nourish our bodies but also whet our appetite for the joyous and abundant banquet you will spread for all peoples. Amen.

Optional Extensions

- Compare and contrast Luke's account with Matthew 14:13-21; Mark 6:30-44; or John 6:1-15. Discuss how similarities and differences highlight different aspects of Jesus and his ministry, and implications for his followers. Why do you think this is the only miracle all four Gospels report?

- Invite someone involved with a ministry, community, or government service that provides food to people facing food insecurity to participate in your group's discussion.

SESSION 4

A Bleeding Woman and a Dead Girl
The Importance of Women's Bodies
(Matthew 9:18-26)

Session Objectives

Through this session's readings and discussion, participants will:

- consider biblical resources for a faithful attitude toward the human body,
- discuss Matthew's "story sandwich" (intercalation) about Jesus's healing of a woman who was bleeding and raising of a girl who had died, and
- identify specific issues in which they could act as advocates for healthy attention to and care for women's bodies.

Biblical Foundations

For it was you who formed my inward parts;
* you knit me together in my mother's womb.*
I praise you, for I am fearfully and wonderfully made.

Wonderful are your works;
that I know very well.
My frame was not hidden from you,
when I was being made in secret,
intricately woven in the depths of the earth.
Psalm 139:13-15

While [Jesus] was saying these things to them, suddenly a leader came and knelt before him, saying, "My daughter has just died; but come and lay your hand on her, and she will live." And Jesus got up and followed him, with his disciples. Then suddenly a woman who had been suffering from hemorrhages for twelve years came up behind him and touched the fringe of his cloak, for she said to herself, "If I only touch his cloak, I will be made well." Jesus turned, and seeing her he said, "Take heart, daughter; your faith has made you well." And instantly the woman was made well. When Jesus came to the leader's house and saw the flute players and the crowd making a commotion, he said, "Go away; for the girl is not dead but sleeping." And they laughed at him. But when the crowd had been put outside, he went in and took her by the hand, and the girl got up. And the report of this spread throughout that district.
Matthew 9:18-26

Before Your Session

- Carefully read chapter 4 of *Signs and Wonders*, noting topics about which you have questions or want to do further research.
- Read this session's Biblical Foundations several times, as well as background information about them from a trusted study Bible or commentary.
- You will need: Bibles for participants and/or on-screen slides, prepared with Scripture texts, to share; for on-site groups, newsprint or a markerboard and markers.
- Lead with sensitivity your group's discussions of physical health and body image. Be ready to direct people toward

physical and mental health resources that can help them address issues these discussions may raise.

Starting Your Session

Welcome participants.

Have participants turn in their Bibles to Psalm 139, and/or share the text on a screen slide. Read the text aloud together. Discuss:

- What does this psalm tell us about how God regards the human body?
- What are this psalm's implications for how human beings should regard their bodies?

Invite volunteers to look up in their Bibles and read aloud these verses: Genesis 1:27 and 2:7; John 1:14; and Romans 12:1. Discuss:

- How do these Scriptures add to our understanding of the human body?
- In your experience, how do Christian faith and practice shape the way people view and treat the human body? Do you think how we understand and appreciate our bodies has to do with our genders?
- How does your congregation encourage and equip people to care for their bodies?

Tell participants that the passage in this session actually includes *two* miracles. Read aloud from *Signs and Wonders*:

> [This story] uses a narrative technique called *intercalation*, which means the sandwiching of one story within another story. Like pastrami on rye, or peanut butter and banana between two pieces of bread fried in butter, the inside receives new flavors because of the outside, and vice versa.

Tell participants today's "story sandwich" raises, among other issues, questions about how God, and how we, care for the human body, specifically women's bodies.

Lead this prayer aloud, or one of your own:

You delight in beauty, O God, and from the dust You lovingly fashioned us for embodied life in Your good creation. Breathe into us again wisdom and understanding, that our reading and discussion today may lead us to see and serve others as whole people, body and soul, for the sake of Jesus, whom we worship as Your Word made flesh. Amen.

Discussion Questions

Exploring Matthew's Story of a Woman Healed and a Girl Raised

Recruit two volunteers to read aloud Matthew 9:18-26, while other participants read along silently. To highlight the "sandwich" structure, have one volunteer read aloud verses 18-19 and 23-26, and the other, verses 20-22. Discuss:

- A leader—better translated "ruler"—kneels before Jesus (verse 18). What does his physical posture show about how he sees his relationship to Jesus? How does your congregation use bodily postures and gestures in worship—sitting, standing, kneeling, genuflection, or others—to express your relationship to God, to Jesus, or to each other?
- "There's a simple lesson" in the ruler's kneeling, AJ suggests: "there are some things we cannot do." When do you find it easy to recognize your limitations and ask for help? When do you find it more difficult? How do you make sure you are heard when you ask? How do you increase your ability to hear others who ask you for help?
- AJ notes the ruler "commands" Jesus to bring his daughter back to life and that "[d]emanding something from the divine is completely consistent with worshipping" (as in psalms of lament, for example). Have you ever demanded

something of God? Do you think of the "Our Father" prayer as composed of imperatives?

- Matthew says Jesus "followed" the ruler (verse 19). "People in Matthew tend to follow Jesus," AJ observes, "so much so that the term 'following' functions...as synonym for 'discipleship'. . . . Jesus never demands anything of his followers that he will not do himself." How is Jesus's body in motion, following this ruler and father, a model of discipleship? Have you ever followed anyone because you want to be a follower of Jesus? Where did they lead you? What did you do there?

- AJ refutes claims, often read in Christian commentaries and heard from Christian pulpits, that the woman breaks Jewish purity laws in approaching Jesus and touching his cloak—as well as claims that Jesus breaks those laws to heal her. How does a mistaken focus on ritual purity distract us from this miracle's significance? How can we see Jesus looking good in this story without making Judaism look bad (as AJ often says)?

- AJ questions the assumption that the woman feels ashamed. When have you or someone you know been shamed for a physical ailment? How does society shame or stigmatize those, especially women, whose "bodies are not behaving well"? What does and what more could your congregation do to welcome and be a shame-free environment for people with physical ailments?

- Why do you imagine the woman doesn't approach Jesus directly, as the dead girl's father did? Do you know any women who, for one reason or another, don't directly ask for what they need? Have you ever hesitated to make your needs known? How do and can communities of faith ask directly for their needs to be met?

- In the NRSV the woman thinks, "I will be made well" (verse 21), but the Greek term, as AJ notes, means "to be saved." "Salvation, in Jewish thought and here in the Gospel as well," writes AJ, "is not primarily something that concerns life after death. Salvation is also life during life." How comfortably does your congregation talk about "salvation" as a present, concrete reality? Does talking about salvation as something to be experienced here and now diminish the importance of an eternal salvation? Why or why not? In your congregation, how is salvation in this life "something that we all can provide to others, if we try"?

- What do you think Jesus implies by addressing the woman as "daughter" (verse 22)? How does this word define her identity? How does it connect this miracle to the one the ruler has asked Jesus to perform? (Refer also to Jesus addressing the man who is paralyzed as "child" in Mark 2:5—refer to Session 1.)

- Jesus tells the woman to "be courageous" or "be confident," reminding us, writes AJ, "that we can be the source of courage and confidence to others." How does your congregation fill this role? How might you fill that role?

- Why does Jesus tell the crowd at the ruler's house the dead girl is sleeping (verses 23-24)? How does a belief in resurrection, which AJ notes "most first-century Jews" held, help us understand his words? (Compare the apostle Paul's use of "sleep" as a metaphor for death in 1 Corinthians 15:6, 18, 51.)

- AJ translates the end of verse 25 literally as "and raised the little girl." How does this verse link Jesus's raising of the girl to both the belief in resurrection and his own resurrection to come?

After discussing the details of the two healing miracles, discuss:

- What does this "story sandwich" add to our earlier discussion about a faithful view of women's bodies, and of all human bodies?

Closing Your Session: Advocating Healthy Attention to Women's Bodies

Read aloud from *Signs and Wonders*, "The dead girl had her father to advocate for her; the woman [who was bleeding] advocates for herself." Tell participants one of the conclusions AJ draws from these stories is "women's bodies, and the problems unique to women's bodies, are just as demanding of and worthy of attention as are men's bodies and the problems unique to men's bodies."

Suggest the followers of Jesus, who care for women's bodies in these (and other) stories, have a special responsibility to advocate for such care today.

Brainstorm with participants a list of issues that demand healthy attentiveness to and care for women's bodies. Should you want to "prime the pump," such a list could include:

- cancer research, prevention, and treatment (for example, breast, ovarian, cervical);
- nutritional deficiencies more likely to affect women (for example, anemia);
- reproductive health;
- domestic abuse;
- mental health issues (for example, postpartum depression, eating disorders); and
- hypersexualized images of women in media

Not every issue on the list affects *only* women (for example, men also have eating disorders; men are also abused). But the implications each issue on the list has for women's bodies should be clear. You might ask the people in your group what issues they wish received more constructive attention (emphasizing you are not asking them to name only issues they personally have faced).

Once your group is finished brainstorming, have the group choose one issue. Work together to identify two or three points the group would want to make as people of faith in a letter to the editor, op-ed, or blog post advocating on behalf of women who face the issue. Courageous participants will want to take the next steps of writing a piece and submitting it to the media or publishing it online.

Close by leading this prayer aloud, or one of your own:

Healing Jesus, born of a woman: You lovingly call us Your children, giving us courage and confidence for the future. Put our bodies in motion so we may follow those who are in need. Make us agents of your salvation here and now, that everybody may experience the fullness of life for which we were created. Amen.

Optional Extensions

- Examine one or both of the other two examples of intercalation AJ mentions—Mark 6:7-34 and Mark 11:12-20—and look for others in the Gospels. How do these "sandwiches" enhance the "taste" of their narrative ingredients and their thematic "flavor"?
- Compare and contrast Matthew's version of these miracles with Mark 5:21-43 and Luke 8:4-56. What details does Matthew omit? Why do you think he did? Which version of these miracles do you most prefer, and why? What wisdom do you find in the New Testament preserving various versions?
- Invite someone who is involved with health and/or social services to women, if not already present, to participate in your discussion.

A Two-Stage Miracle
Seeing Again
(Mark 8:22-26)

Session Objectives

Through this session's readings and discussion, participants will:

- experience some visual "blind spots" and misconceptions, and think about figurative "blind spots" of their own,
- read and reflect on Mark's account of Jesus's two-stage miracle in the context of the disciples' failures to "see" Jesus clearly (Mark 8:14-33), and
- identify people for whom their congregation could help cultivate an "open future."

Biblical Foundation

Now the disciples had forgotten to bring any bread; and they had only one loaf with them in the boat. And [Jesus] cautioned them, saying, "Watch out—beware of the yeast of the Pharisees and the yeast of Herod." They said to one another, "It is because we have no bread." And becoming aware of it, Jesus said to them, "Why are you talking about having no bread? Do you still not perceive or understand? Are your hearts hardened? Do you have eyes, and fail to see? Do you have ears, and fail to hear? And do you not remember? When I broke the five loaves for the five thousand, how many baskets full of broken pieces did you collect?" They said to him, "Twelve." "And the seven for the four thousand, how many baskets full of broken pieces did you collect?" And they said to him, "Seven." Then he said to them, "Do you not yet understand?"

They came to Bethsaida. Some people brought a blind man to him and begged him to touch him. He took the blind man by the hand and led him out of the village; and when he had put saliva on his eyes and laid his hands on him, he asked him, "Can you see anything?" And the man looked up and said, "I can see people, but they look like trees, walking." Then Jesus laid his hands on his eyes again; and he looked intently and his sight was restored, and he saw everything clearly. Then he sent him away to his home, saying, "Do not even go into the village."

Jesus went on with his disciples to the villages of Caesarea Philippi; and on the way he asked his disciples, "Who do people say that I am?" And they answered him, "John the Baptist; and others, Elijah; and still others, one of the prophets." He asked them, "But who do you say that I am?" Peter answered him, "You are the Messiah." And he sternly ordered them not to tell anyone about him.

Then he began to teach them that the Son of Man must undergo great suffering, and be rejected by the elders, the chief priests, and the scribes, and be killed, and after three days rise again. He said all this quite openly. And Peter took him aside and began to rebuke him. But turning and looking at his disciples, he rebuked Peter and said, "Get behind me, Satan! For you are setting your mind not on divine things but on human things."

Mark 8:14-33

Before Your Session

- Carefully read chapter 5 of *Signs and Wonders*, noting topics about which you have questions or want to do further research.

- Read this session's Biblical Foundation several times, as well as background information about it from a trusted study Bible or commentary.
- You will need: Bibles for participants and/or on-screen slides, prepared with Scripture texts, to share; on-site groups will need newsprint or a markerboard and markers.
- *Optional*: Find an online "blind spot" test and/or optical illusion to share with your group. You can send a link to the "blind spot" test to participants in an email, via text message, or (if meeting virtually or in hybrid format) in your videoconferencing platform's chat feature. You can also send links to optical illusions, or print them to display.

Starting Your Session

Welcome participants.

Optional: Following AJ's suggests in chapter 5 to ask willing participants to take one of the "blind spot" tests available online for fun. (See suggestions above for sharing links to the test.) Alternatively or in addition, display a few optical illusions to your group. Invite participants to describe their experiences of these "tests" of vision and perception. (You may want to replace or supplement this activity with another if some participants cannot take part because of visual impairments.)

Read aloud this statement from *Signs and Wonders*: "Seeing clearly is an art." Discuss:

- When do you have the most trouble physically seeing clearly?
- When was a time you have thought, "I can't believe my eyes"?
- When was a time you missed seeing something others thought you should have seen?

- When have you "seen" something positive about another person they were unwilling or unable to "see" about themselves? How, if at all, did you help them see it? When has someone done the same for you?
- What are some personal, figurative "blind spots" you know you have? How do you strive to adjust for them so you can "see" more clearly?
- What risks do we run when using vision and sight as metaphors for understanding? What other language could we use?

Tell participants the miracle story in this session will, as AJ suggests, challenge us to identify some of our own, metaphorical "blind spots" about Jesus and about our own strengths and weaknesses as his followers.

Lead this prayer aloud, or one of your own:

O God, who fashioned the ear, do You not hear? O God, who formed the eye, do You not see? You know our thoughts cannot ever reach Yours, but in grace You call us to listen to Your wisdom and seek Your ways, that we may know enough to do your will. Guide our study in this time, granting us new insights into Your power and Your purpose, and showing us how much You would still have us learn as we follow the way of Jesus Christ. Amen.

Discussion Questions

Discussing Disciples' Failures to "See" Jesus Clearly

Tell participants that while the narrative context of all the miracle stories matters, what precedes and follows this session's story can be especially informative.

Recruit a volunteer to read aloud Mark 8:14-21, while other participants read along silently. Discuss:

- What do you think Jesus means when he cautions his disciples about "the yeast of the Pharisees and the yeast of

Herod" (verse 15; see also 8:11-12)? What do the disciples think he means (verses 14, 16)?

- With what tone of voice do you imagine Jesus asking his disciples the questions he does, and why (verses 17-21)?
- How does this episode illustrate the disciples' "blind spots" about Jesus?

Now recruit a volunteer to read aloud Mark 8:27-33, while other participants read along silently. Discuss:

- Why does Jesus ask the disciples who other people say he is (verse 27) before asking them for their opinion (verse 29)?
- AJ notes verse 30 contains a "motif" (recurring pattern) in Mark known as "the messianic secret." "The Gospel does not tell us why Jesus is not interested in publicity," AJ writes, "which sounds initially counter-intuitive to a mission designed to get people to repent and believe the kingdom is at hand." Why do you think Jesus would want his messianic identity kept secret?
- What does Jesus say "quite openly" about his identity (verses 31-32)? Why does Peter rebuke him for it (verse 32)? Why does Jesus rebuke Peter (verse 33)?
- How does this episode illustrate Peter's "blind spots" about Jesus?

Taking a Close Look at Jesus's Two-Stage Miracle

Recruit three volunteers to read aloud Mark 8:22-26, taking the "roles" of the narrator, Jesus, and the man Jesus heals. Discuss:

- Who do you imagine brings this man to Jesus? Why do they plead with Jesus to touch him? Have you ever pleaded with God on anyone's behalf? Why? What happened? How do and can communities of faith help people cultivate more of the empathy on display as this story begins?

- AJ wonders whether Jesus led the man out of the village (verse 23) because "he feared [the healing] would not work." What do you think? AJ finds a Jesus who appears "weak, or even doubtful," a relatable and comforting Jesus. Do you? Why or why not?
- How do you react to what some of AJ's students have called "the icky part" of the miracle, Jesus spitting on the man's eyes (verse 23)? How does knowing Roman stories about the Emperor Vespasian's healing saliva inform your understanding of this detail? Does reflecting on the intimate sharing of a bodily fluid—"kissing a boo-boo," in AJ's words—change your understanding of what Jesus does?
- Jesus also touches the man, as those who brought the man to him wanted him to do. "[I]n many human settings," writes AJ, "the touch of another is sustaining, even healing. We learn with our bodies; we feel with our flesh. We need that physical contact." Whose physical touch has sustained and healed you? Whom have you sustained and healed through your touch?
- Why does Jesus ask the man whether the man sees anything (verse 23)? With what tone of voice do you imagine he asks it? How might this question echo his questions to his disciples in the episodes before and after this miracle story?
- "The man was able to distinguish what he saw from what he knew he should see," writes AJ. "He knew there was something not quite right about what he saw. The harder move is for those of us who have pretty good sight to realize what we are seeing is incomplete." How do we make that realization? What can we do to check and correct our vision—literal and otherwise—when we need

to? How can communities of faith encourage clear sight about "things [that] are not the way they should be"?

- Read Isaiah 29:18-21. How does Jesus's restoration of sight to this man connect to the "perfection of the body" AJ says was "among the more popular" first-century Jewish expectations for the messianic age? In what other ways do Isaiah's words anticipate the "perfection" of the messianic? Which aspects seem particularly urgent to you today, and why?

- "Jewish messianic expectations for the most part did not think of the messiah as performing healings," writes AJ. How might John the Baptizer's questions about Jesus's identity (Matthew 11:2-6; Luke 7:18-23) reflect these expectations? If Jesus's identity "has to be discerned," as AJ argues the Gospels claim, how can and does the church help people, both within and beyond its membership, discern his identity now?

- How might Jesus's final instructions to the man (verse 26) reflect the "messianic secret" motif? AJ implies that Mark is suggesting that "we not focus on Jesus's ability to perform miracles; instead, we should focus on what has happened to him, and so to us." What difference does this distinction make for Christian faith and practice?

- How do the episodes on either side of this miracle story, studied earlier in this session, help us understand it as a story about discerning Jesus's identity?

Closing Your Session:
Fostering Open Futures as Jesus's Followers

Read aloud from *Signs and Wonders*:

The person who left [Bethsaida] is not the same as the person who returned. Just as the man, now with perfect sight, has to adjust to his new life, so will his friends and family. The future is open.

Invite participants to imagine for a few minutes the specifics of this "open future." Ask when, if ever, they have experienced a similarly open future in their lives. Ask who and what made that open future possible.

Suggest that part of "seeing" Jesus more clearly could be following his example and doing what we can to foster "open futures" for those who need them.

Distribute newspapers and magazines. Instruct participants to find a news article about people who need an open future. (Participants may also search reputable news sources online.) Ask some volunteers to talk about the articles they select with the whole group, explaining how they think your congregation does or could contribute to encouraging an open future in these situations.

Close by leading this prayer aloud, or one of your own:

Show us, loving God, the neighbors near or far whom You would have us serve by giving our time, our treasure, and our talents for the sake of their open future. Increase our desire to discern more clearly what it means for us to call Your Son "Messiah," that we may also know more fully whom You have created and call us to be. Amen.

Optional Extensions

- AJ notes this miracle story could be Mark's "riff" on the Allegory of the Cave from Plato's *Republic*. Invite someone, before your session, to research Plato's story; or find a brief and accurate video about it online that your group could watch during the session. Compare and contrast the two stories. AJ says Mark's conclusion is that Jesus, not philosophy, reveals truth. Of what value, if any, is non-Christian philosophy to Christians, and why?
- Invite someone who works (professionally or on a volunteer basis) as an advocate for people with physical disabilities to participate in your discussion.

SESSION 6

The Raising of Lazarus
Taking Death Seriously
(John 11:1-44)

Session Objectives

Through this session's readings and discussion, participants will:

- talk about some of their feelings about death;
- read and discuss most of John 11, focusing on how the chapter attends to issues of sickness, death, and new life; and
- review personal and group highlights from this study and ponder together what differences belief in miracles can make to faith and practice.

Biblical Foundation

Now a certain man was ill, Lazarus of Bethany, the village of Mary and her sister Martha. Mary was the one who anointed the Lord with perfume and wiped his feet with her hair; her brother Lazarus was ill. So the sisters sent a message to Jesus, "Lord, he whom you love is ill." But when Jesus heard it, he said, "This illness does not lead to death; rather it is for God's glory, so that the Son of God may be glorified through it." Accordingly, though Jesus loved Martha and her sister and

The Raising of Lazarus

Lazarus, after having heard that Lazarus was ill, he stayed two days longer in the place where he was....

[Jesus said to his disciples,] "Our friend Lazarus has fallen asleep, but I am going there to awaken him." The disciples said to him, "Lord, if he has fallen asleep, he will be all right." Jesus, however, had been speaking about his death, but they thought that he was referring merely to sleep. Then Jesus told them plainly, "Lazarus is dead. For your sake I am glad I was not there, so that you may believe. But let us go to him."...

Now Bethany was near Jerusalem, some two miles away, and many of the Jews had come to Martha and Mary to console them about their brother. When Martha heard that Jesus was coming, she went and met him, while Mary stayed at home. Martha said to Jesus, "Lord, if you had been here, my brother would not have died. But even now I know that God will give you whatever you ask of him." Jesus said to her, "Your brother will rise again." Martha said to him, "I know that he will rise again in the resurrection on the last day." Jesus said to her, "I am the resurrection and the life. Those who believe in me, even though they die, will live, and everyone who lives and believes in me will never die. Do you believe this?" She said to him, "Yes, Lord, I believe that you are the Messiah, the Son of God, the one coming into the world."

When she had said this, she went back and called her sister Mary, and told her privately, "The Teacher is here and is calling for you." And when she heard it, she got up quickly and went to him.... When Mary came where Jesus was and saw him, she knelt at his feet and said to him, "Lord, if you had been here, my brother would not have died." When Jesus saw her weeping, and the Jews who came with her also weeping, he was greatly disturbed in spirit and deeply moved. He said, "Where have you laid him?" They said to him, "Lord, come and see." Jesus began to weep....

Then Jesus, again greatly disturbed, came to the tomb. It was a cave, and a stone was lying against it. Jesus said, "Take away the stone." Martha, the sister of the dead man, said to him,

"Lord, already there is a stench because he has been dead four days." Jesus said to her, "Did I not tell you that if you believed, you would see the glory of God?"... [Jesus] cried with a loud voice, "Lazarus, come out!" The dead man came out, his hands and feet bound with strips of cloth, and his face wrapped in a cloth. Jesus said to them, "Unbind him, and let him go."

John 11:1-6, 11-15, 18-29, 32-35, 38-40, 43-44

Before Your Session

- Carefully read chapter 6 and the conclusion of *Signs and Wonders*, noting topics about which you have questions or want to do further research.
- Read this session's Biblical Foundation several times, as well as background information about it from a trusted study Bible or commentary.
- You will need: Bibles for participants and/or on-screen slides, prepared with Scripture texts, to share; on-site groups will need newsprint or a markerboard and markers.
- Discussing death may be difficult for people who are grieving, depressed, or struggling with suicidal thoughts. Be ready to help people who need emergency resources get them. Ask pastoral leadership or local mental health professionals for help, and share information about such national helplines as:
  - ◊ *National Suicide Prevention Lifeline:* 1-800-273-8255 (1-800-273-TALK); https://suicidepreventionlifeline.org/
  - ◊ *National Hopeline Network* (serving students and young adults): 1-800-442-4673; https://www.thehopeline.com/
  - ◊ *National Alliance on Mental Illness:* 1-800-950-NAMI (6264); https://www.nami.org/help

Starting Your Session

Welcome participants.

Tell participants the final miracle story your group will consider is Jesus's raising of Lazarus, recounted in John 11. Tell them AJ writes that she appreciates this chapter "because it takes the time to think about death.... Death has both general and particular impacts. We do not all approach it the same way, nor should we be expected to do so." Discuss:

- What is your earliest memory of dealing with death? How have your feelings about that experience changed over the years?
- In our culture, how well or poorly do we take time to think about death? Why? What about in our congregation?
- What rituals and traditions does your congregation practice to help survivors when someone dies?
- How comfortable are you thinking about your own mortality? Why?
- How can we avoid spending too little or too much time thinking about death? Who can help us when we have troubling thoughts about death?

Lead this prayer aloud, or one of your own:

Eternal God, You alone are immortal. As we face the mystery of death in our study today, comfort us, by Your Spirit, with Your presence. Strengthen us to speak honestly with each other and with You. Heighten our ability to hear Your word of love and life. Move us to respond with ever greater faithfulness to him who weeps with us in the face of death, yet is for us the resurrection and eternal life today, Jesus Christ. Amen.

Discussion Questions

Discussing Death and New Life in John 11

Recruit several volunteers to read aloud John 11 while others read along silently. If time allows, you may want to read the entire chapter; however, tell participants your discussion will follow AJ's lead of focusing on portions "that address sickness and death and then new life."

Discuss:

- What does Mary and Martha's message to Jesus (verse 3) suggest about their relationship with Jesus?
- AJ writes: "The illness of a loved one can divide a family; it can also unite them." When, if ever, have you experienced family division or reconciliation in connection with a family member's sickness? How does or could your congregation minister to families dealing with a loved one's illness?
- How do you react to Jesus's delaying his departure for Bethany (verses 4-6)?
- "Yes," writes AJ, "it's okay to be annoyed, or upset, or even angered by a biblical passage." How much do you agree or disagree, and why? Has "wrestling" with a biblical passage as AJ describes ever led you to a new understanding or to take new action in faith? How?
- AJ says she'd prefer to "rephrase the storyline: people do not suffer *so that* divine glory can be revealed," then mentions how she sees divine glory in other people's responses to those who suffer. What specific examples from your own or others' experience can you provide?
- Why does Jesus use "sleep" as a euphemism for death (verse 11)? What euphemisms have you heard for death? When are these figures of speech helpful, and when are they not?

- Commenting on the disciples' response to Jesus's euphemism (verses 12-13), AJ writes, "On the one hand, the disciples have no clue what they are saying; on the other hand, they are exactly right, at least in John's perspective." How does this irony enhance this story's effect(s) and clarify its meaning(s)?

- Why do you think John mentions that Lazarus has been in the tomb for four days (verses 17, 39)?

- AJ mentions that, in chapters 12–21, John's Gospel increasingly associates the Greek *Ioudaioi* ("the Jews") with "the world that rejects Jesus." Why does she appreciate John's notice that "the Jews" are consoling Mary and Martha (verse 19)? Why does death have power to bring people of "decidedly different views" together? When have you seen it do so?

- Martha and Mary's different reactions to Jesus's arrival (verse 20) indicate "no single approach is necessarily right" in times of grief, AJ writes. How do you tend to process your "strong emotions"? How do you react to displays of strong emotions, such as grief, by others? Have your tendencies and reactions changed over time?

- Martha assumes Jesus is referring to a future, "general resurrection of the dead" when he tells her Lazarus will rise (verses 23-24). But she "wants Lazarus with her now," writes AJ, "not at the end of the ages." When, if ever, have you or has someone you know found doctrine insufficient in the face of grief? How does or should this experience inform the way we talk to and care for people who are grieving?

- How does Jesus reframe belief in the resurrection (verses 25-26)? "The point need not be theologically abstract," AJ writes. What are some tangible, "palpable" ways have you sensed new life in the midst of this life?

- AJ points out Martha's confession of faith in Jesus (verse 27) "is not only more detailed" than Peter's in Mark 8:29 (see session 5) but also apparently "based on less evidence." "She believes," writes AJ, "and she does so because there's something about Jesus that she trusts." How does Martha exemplify John's ideal reader (20:31)? If you believe John's claims about Jesus, why?

- In what tones do you hear Mary and Martha speaking their initial, identical words to Jesus (verses 21, 32)? Why? What significance do you find in this repeated question? Have you ever asked Jesus or God this question yourself?

- "The idea of the divine weeping together with humanity in the face of death is part of Jesus's culture," AJ writes. Why does AJ argue against making emotions "the major indication of humanity vs. divinity"? What other Bible stories witness to God's emotions? How do you react to the idea that God weeps with humanity?

- How do we read Jesus's words to Martha in verse 40 in ways that avoid, as AJ says, "false hope and bad religion"—the idea that "we have failed because our belief is not strong enough"? How might John's emphasis on "signs"—supernatural actions that can *lead* to trust in Jesus—rather than Matthew, Mark, and Luke's "miracles"—supernatural actions that *follow* trust in him—help us?

- Commenting on Jesus's call to Lazarus (verse 43), AJ writes, "When we feel dead inside—from social expectations, parental desires, workplace demands, whatever—this call is an affirmation." Do you know or know of anyone who has responded to Jesus's call to "come out" from death into a new life? How do or could you and your congregation support people coming out of whatever "binds" them?

Closing Your Session:
Moving Into Miraculous New Possibilities

Thank your group for their participation and engagement in this study of *Signs and Wonders*. Tell them one or two key things you will remember from your study together, and invite volunteers to talk briefly about what they have appreciated most about reading and discussing these miracle stories together.

Read aloud from *Signs and Wonders*:

> [The Gospels' miracle stories] tell us that Jesus does what God does. But there is no reason to stop there. Jesus also models for anyone closely reading the Gospels what we can do.

Discuss:

- What have we seen characters *other* than Jesus in these stories do that we could do, as well? How can these actions be "acts of salvation"?
- "There may be miracle workers in places, even in our own families, that we had never realized," writes AJ. Who are these "miracle workers" in your life? How did they position you to enter an open future with new possibilities? What can and will you do to honor the miracles they have worked for or within you?
- "If we do perceive something to be a miracle," writes AJ, "then the test for viability should be the answer to the question, 'So what?' How does believing in a miracle…change your life?" Having finished this study of *Signs and Wonders*, how do you answer that question?

Close by leading this prayer aloud, or one of your own:

Make us more alert to miracles, O God—not that we may be startled by spectacle, not that we may have "proof" of Your power or our faith, but that we may grow and change in our view of ourselves, of Your world, and of the future You open for us; that we may move, moment by moment, farther into Your realm where all things are possible, for ourselves and for others. Amen.

Optional Extension

- Several times in chapter 6, AJ references the New Testament's other story about Mary and Martha, Luke 10:38-42. Read this story and compare and contrast its characterizations of the sisters with those in John 11. How does each story help you better understand the other?